Toys Save the Train

Published by Scholastic Inc., *Publishers since 1920*. SCHOLASTIC and associated logos
are trademarks and/or registered trademarks of Scholastic Inc. All rights reserved.

The publisher does not have any control over and does not assume
any responsibility for author or third-party websites or their content.

This book is a work of fiction. Names, characters, places, and incidents are either the product of the
author's imagination or are used fictitiously, and any resemblance to actual persons, living or dead,
business establishments, events, or locales is entirely coincidental.

ISBN: 978-1-338-57289-6

10 9 8 7 6 5 4 3 2 1   19 20 21 22 23

Printed in Malaysia   106

First printing, 2019

Book design by Marissa Asuncion

Scholastic Inc.

Sheriff Woody sees a **train**.
He knows there is money
on that **train**.

Ka-blam! A bad guy blows up the money car on the **train**! Woody **races** after it.

Woody sees a bad guy.
"Stop in the **name**
of the law," says Woody.

"Never!" says the bad guy. "You are too **late**! This **train** is headed off the **rails**!"

A bad guy pushes Woody.
He falls off the **train**!

Jessie **races** to help him!
She **saves** Woody.

Now Woody and Jessie have to stop the **train**. Woody leaps to the first car.

He pulls the **brake**.
But he is too **late**!
He cannot stop the **train**.

The **train** jumps a **rail**
and runs off the track!

Is this the end of the line
for Woody?

Look! It is Buzz,
the flying **space** man.
Buzz **saves** the **train**!

Now the three friends
can **take** on the bad guys.
The **chase** is on!

The bad guys do not **wait**.
They **race** off in their car.

The friends **chase** the car.
Buzz **aims** his **laser** and shoots!
He stops the car.

Woody and his friends
catch the bad guys.
They **save** the **day**!